# traditional art of the african nations

# traditional art of the african nations

IN THE MUSEUM OF PRIMITIVE ART

*with an Introduction by Robert Goldwater*

*and photographs by Charles Uht*

THE MUSEUM OF PRIMITIVE ART, NEW YORK. DISTRIBUTED BY UNIVERSITY PUBLISHERS INC., NEW YORK 1961

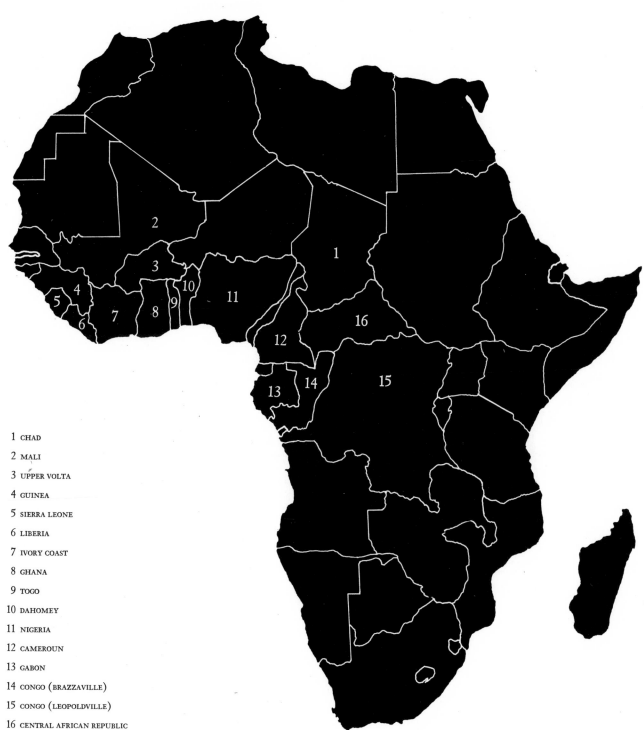

1 CHAD

2 MALI

3 UPPER VOLTA

4 GUINEA

5 SIERRA LEONE

6 LIBERIA

7 IVORY COAST

8 GHANA

9 TOGO

10 DAHOMEY

11 NIGERIA

12 CAMEROUN

13 GABON

14 CONGO (BRAZZAVILLE)

15 CONGO (LEOPOLDVILLE)

16 CENTRAL AFRICAN REPUBLIC

# introduction

On the continent of Africa a group of nations has emerged. Recently organized, recently independent, the rest of the world has become accustomed to think of them as the new nations of Africa. And so they are in the limited sense of geographical identity and political structure.

But in another, more profound sense these nations are far from new, or even recent arrivals. Socially, culturally, aesthetically, their peoples have a long and intricate history. Since for the most part that history has been orally transmitted, we know only a portion, probably only a small portion of the complex of its traditions and development. Some few specific dates have been recorded by travellers from abroad; others, more ancient, have been revealed by archaeology, which has told us enough so that we may be sure that further investigations will tell us much more; some oral histories are apparently chronologically accurate. But there are not many such temporally pin-pointed facts, and their scarcity has perhaps given them an undue importance, compared to the vast totality of African cultural history.

Even without documents, we can infer the quality of this history from what we know of the nature of the recent past. The many cultural traditions of Africa, in all their distinction and variety, the ordering of their social structure, the intricacy and sharpness of their religious beliefs, the wealth of their oral traditions—all these can only have evolved in the course of a long, complex and thoughtful history.

The plastic arts of Africa are a manifestation of this cultural history, the one perhaps best known to the world in general, and they carry its evidence within themselves. Their skilled technique has a directness that comes from an almost intuitive use of established methods, passed on and gradually perfected. Their styles are as various as the cultures that have developed them, since they embody and externalize them. Because the cultural unit has been the "tribe" (which may number many hundreds of thousands of persons and so is perhaps better referred to as a people), and the art reflects this unit, any one of today's nations has been the home of many styles. If these styles are distinct and recognizable, they are also related, and have influenced and borrowed from each other. Neither immutable nor isolated, yet clearly formed and individual, they are like the arts of the city-states of Italy —Florence, Siena, or Bologna—each having its separate style (marginally affected by trade and travel), and all the product of related vision.

The traditional arts of Africa's nations are then, in their own right, old arts. This remains true even though because of the perishable materials so widely employed only a minority of the works known to us are of any great historical age. Function, whether symbolic or magic, was paramount, and antiquity as such had little meaning for the original intention of these arts.

Yet there are two senses in which African art as illustrated here from the collections of The Museum of Primitive Art may be said to be new: one stems from understanding, the other from knowledge.

During the last few years we have come to know of the existence of hitherto unsuspected styles and of a whole wide range of individual works—some of them masterpieces. In a few instances these are in fact recent styles; in most, however, it is our knowledge,

rather than the works, which is new. The total impact has been a new realization of the richness and variety of African sculpture.

The relation of African art to modern Western art and the few important instances of strong influence, are by now familiar. Both anthropologists and artists played a role in first seeing and then collecting, but it was crucially the freer vision propagated by the painters and sculptors that permitted the modern eye to receive the shock and impact of an unfamiliar art. This new appreciation was highly subjective, yet it was an indispensable step in the direction of the more objective, more understanding enjoyment that has become widespread in the last few years. Thus, for Americans and Europeans African art has entered a new phase—new, that is, for them. It is one which, because it is now based on a maturity of vision to match the maturity of the art, will continue and grow.

ROBERT GOLDWATER

*With the exception of the works from Benin, which were made between the 16th and 18th centuries; and the Kissi heads, which may be prior to 1800, most of the objects in this book are thought to have been made in the last one hundred and fifty years.*

# chad

1   Female figure. Chad: Kenga. Wood, yellow paint, metal band, nails, 11⅞″ high. 56.350

# mali

2  Food vessel. Mali: Dogon. Wood, metal staples, 33¾″ high. 60.39

*3* Hippopotamus. Mali: Dogon. Wood, 20½ʺ long. 59.284

4  Ancestor figure. Mali: Dogon. Wood, 82⅞″ high. 58.97

5 Housepost. Mali, Bandiagara district? Dogon. Wood, 74¼″ high. 58.328

6  Mask. Mali: Dogon. Wood, 43⅜″ high.
61.5

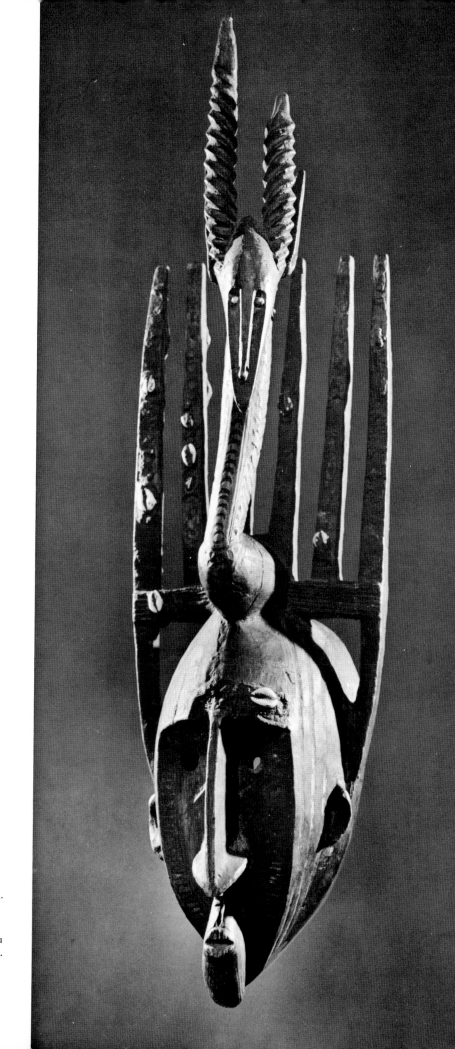

Left: *7* Musicians. Mali: Dogon. Wood, 15½″ high.
59.181

Right: *8* Boy's initiation mask (N'tomo). Mali, Segou
district: Bambara. Wood, shell, seeds, latex, 29″ high.
59.286

9 Female fertility figure. Mali, Bamako
district: Bambara. Wood, brass tacks,
thread ornaments, 24½″ high. 56.223

10 Mask. Mali: Bambara, Marka style. Wood, brass strips, blue paint, red cotton, 11⅜″ high. 59.186

*11*  Ancestral figure. Mali, Bougouni district: Bambara. Wood, 48⅜″ high. 59.110

# upper volta

12 Mask (Do). Upper Volta: Bobo. Wood;
black, white and terra cotta paint; twine; 72″
high. 57.179

Right: *14*  Mask. Upper Volta: Bobo. Wood; black, terra cotta and white paint; 14⅛″ high. 60.116

Below: *13*  Mask. Upper Volta: Bobo. Wood; white, red and black paint; braided rope; 51¼″ wide. 60.167

Right: *16* Mask. Upper Volta: Mossi. Wood, black and white paint, 30⅜″ high. 58.322

Below: *15* Seat. Upper Volta: Bobo. Wood, 22⅛″ high. 60.34

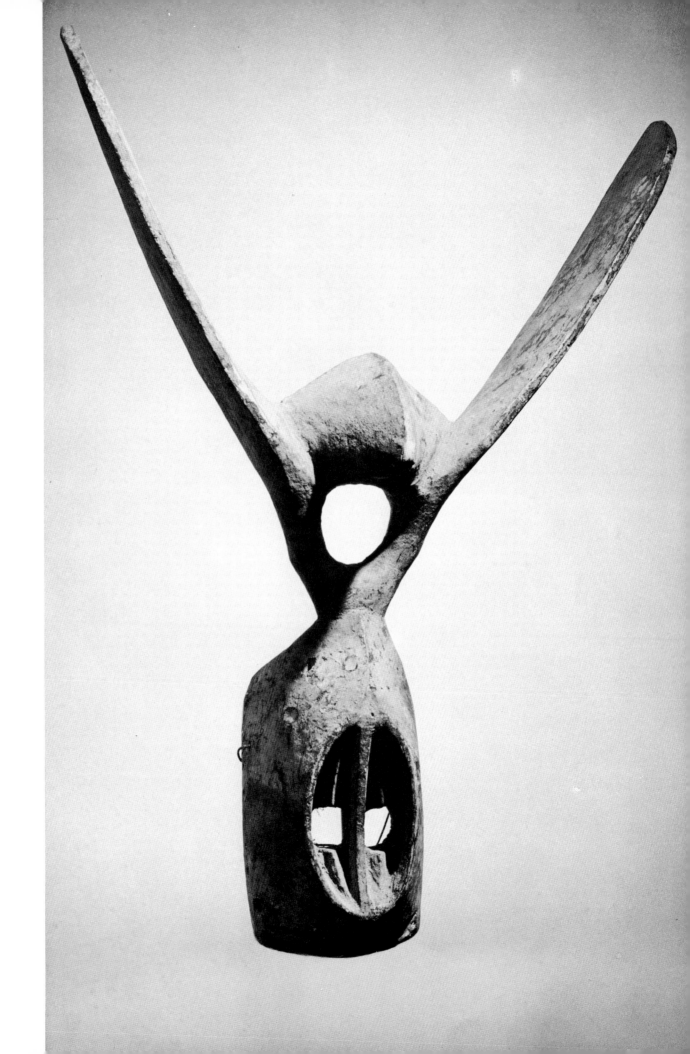

# guinea

Preceding page: *17* Antelope headdress. Upper Volta, Aribinda region: Mossi, Kurumba Society. Wood; blue, black, white, terra cotta, umber and orange paint; iron staples; nails; twine; 45¼″ high. 60.19

Below: *18* Head (Elek). Guinea: Baga. Wood, 31⅝″ high. 57.107

Following pages left: *19* Headdress (Nimba). Guinea: Baga, Simo Society. Wood, 46½″ high. 56.261

Right: *20* Serpents (Kakilambe). Guinea: Baga. Wood; black, white and terra cotta paint; 54½″ high, 58.336; 68½″ high, 58.335. *Photograph by Elisabeth G. Little*

21, 21a   Head. Guinea: Kissi. Stone, 6⅜" long. 61.22

# sierra leone

22   Head. Sierra Leone: Kissi. Stone, 10¼" high. 60.35

# liberia

23 Mask. Liberia: N'gere. Wood; orange, blue and white paint; red fabric; tin; cotton cord; fibre, cloth and wooden ornaments; nails; cartridge cases; 12½″ high. 56.215

Below: *24*  Mask. Liberia: Dan. Wood, cord, hair, iron nail, clay, red paint, 8⅛″ high. 59.260

Right: *25*  Headdress. Ivory Coast: Senufo. Wood, paint, 55⅜″ high. 60.16

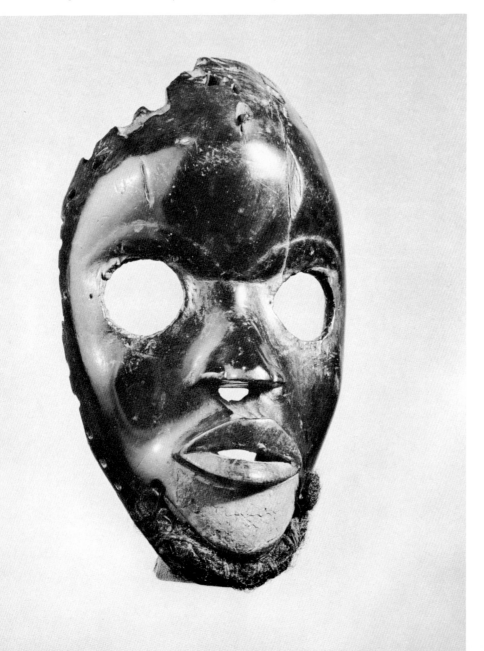

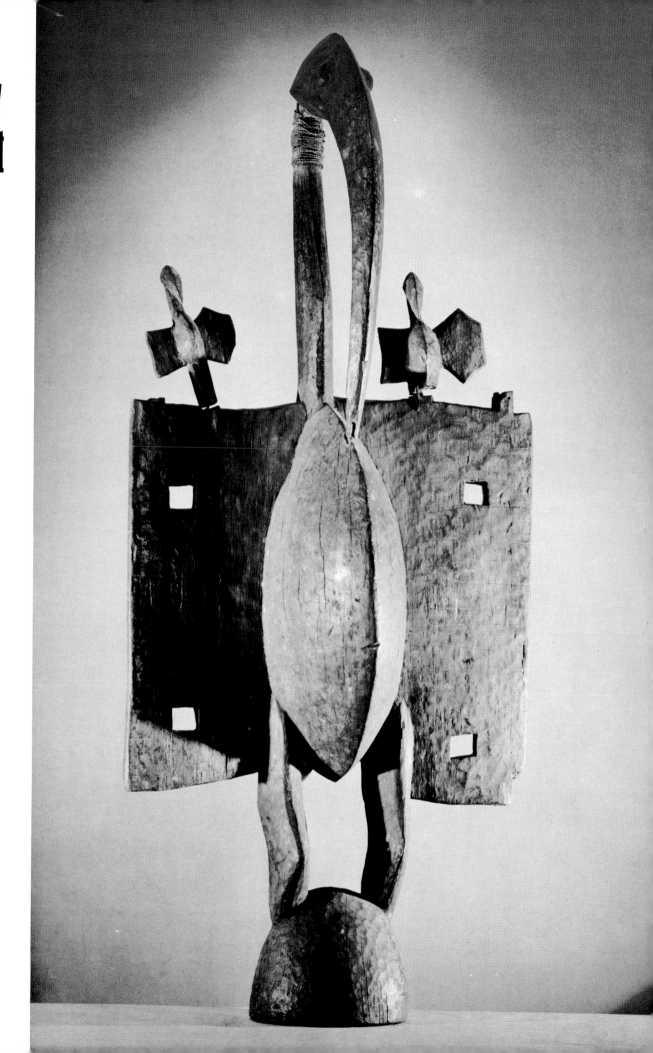

ivory
coast

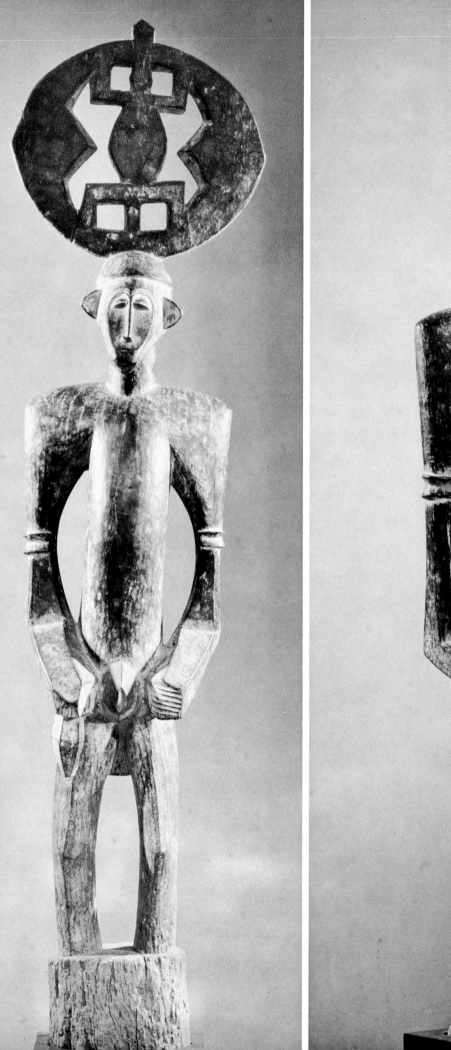

Far left: *26* Ancestor figure: rhythm marker. Ivory Coast: Senufo. Wood, red and white paint, 45⅜″ high. 61.24

Left: *27* Ancestor figure: rhythm marker. Ivory Coast: Senufo. Wood, red and white paint, 38⅛″ high. 61.25

Right: *28* Ancestor figure: rhythm marker. Ivory Coast, Korhogo district, Lataha: Senufo-Tyembara. Wood, 42½″ high. 58.7

Left: *29*  Mask. Ivory Coast: Senufo. Wood, traces of white and terra cotta paint, 16″ high. 59.293

Right: *30*  Container. Ivory Coast: Senufo. Wood, traces of white paint, 13″ high. 60.59

Left: *31*  Mask. Ivory Coast: Senufo. Bronze, 8¼″ high. 61.37

Right: *32*  Mask. Ivory Coast: Guro. Wood, red and black paint, 17⅜″ high. EL 114.61. Extended loan from Mrs. Gertrud A. Mellon

Left: *33* Female figure. Ivory Coast: Guro. Wood, white paint, beads, 25⅞″ high. 59.23

Right: *34* Female figure. Ivory Coast: Baule. Wood, white paint, red and white beads, iron, 20⅝″ high. 60.85

Far right: *35* Male figure. Ivory Coast: Baule. Wood; traces of white paint; blue, black, ochre and red beads; 21¾″ high. 60.84

43759

Left: *36*  Female figure. Ivory Coast: Baule. Wood, glass beads, white paint, 18⅛" high. 56.365

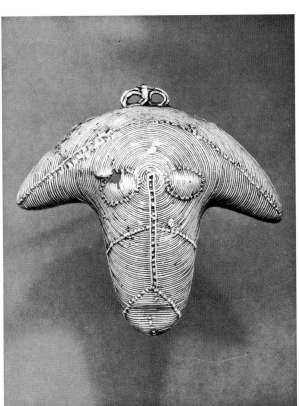

38

39

40

41

Above: *38* Gold-weight. Ivory Coast: Baule. Brass, 4⅛″ high. 60.133

*39* Ring: scorpion. Ivory Coast: Baule. Gold, 2⅛″ long. 59.304

*40* Animal mask. Ivory Coast: Baule. Gold, 3⅜″ high. 56.398

*41* Gold-weight. Ivory Coast: Baule. Brass, 3⅜″ high. 60.132

Left: *37* Pendant mask. Ivory Coast: Baule. Gold, 3½″ high. 60.37

Following page, left: *42* Ape deity (Mbotumbo). Ivory Coast: Baule. Wood, iron, bronze, reed, cotton, 32¾″ high. 58.321

Right: *43* Animal mask. Ivory Coast: Baule. Wood; black, terra cotta and white paint; 34⅛″ high. 58.349.
Gift of Mr. and Mrs. Ben Heller

Left: *44*  Seated figure. Ivory Coast: Baule. Wood, 20″ high. 61.36

Below: *45*  Flute player. Ivory Coast: Krinjabo. Clay, 10⅜″ high. 60.106

Left: 46  Female figure. Ivory Coast, Dabakala: Baule. Wood, traces of white and terra cotta paint, 23" high. 60.130

Right: 47  Mask. Ghana. Wood; black, white and terra cotta paint; 91" high. 60.168

ghana

Below left: *48* Gold dust container (Kuduo). Ghana: Ashanti. Bronze, 6½″ high. 60.72

Below right: *49* Gold dust container (Kuduo). Ghana: Ashanti. Bronze, 10⅜″ high. 60.69

Right: *50* Funerary head. Ghana: Ashanti. Clay, 12⅜″ high. 59.241

**togo**

51    Water-buffalo head. Togo. Clay, 9″ high. 56.36

52    Staff. Dahomey, Abomey. Silver over wood, 24⅞″ high. 57.257
53    Staff. Dahomey. Wood and iron, 19½″ high. 60.87. Gift of Mr. and Mrs. Arthur A. Cohen

52                                        53

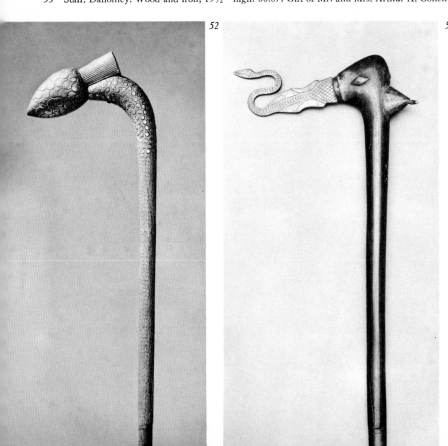

**dahomey**

# nigeria

Left: *54*  Mask. Nigeria, Benin: Bini. Ivory,
iron, copper, stone, 9⅜″ high. 58.100

*55*  Plaque. Nigeria, Benin: Bini. Bronze,
19½″ high. 57.231

Left: *56*   Horn player. Nigeria, Benin: Bini. Bronze, 24⅞″ high. 57.255

Below: *57*   Leopard. Nigeria, Benin: Bini. Bronze, 15¾″ long. 58.90

Left: *58* Guardian spirit (Ejiri). Nigeria: Western Ijo. Wood, traces of black and white paint, 25½″ high. 60.128. Gift of the Matthew T. Mellon Foundation

Below: *59* Bell. Nigeria, Lower Niger area. Bronze, 7⅞″ high. 61.21

Right: *60* Female figure. Nigeria: Ibibio. Wood, black and white paint, 28⅜″ high. 60.127. Gift of the Matthew T. Mellon Foundation

Left: *61* Maternity figure. Nigeria: Yoruba. Wood, traces of red and black paint, 28½″ high. 56.220

Right: *62* Mask. Nigeria: Ibibio. Wood, black and white paint, matting, 22⅜″ high. 59.32

# cameroun

Left: *64*  Head. Cameroun: Bamum? Wood, 22⅞″ high. 57.301. Gift of Mrs. Gertrud A. Mellon

Right: *65*  Drinking horn. Cameroun: Bamum. Horn; red, blue, yellow and white beads, 16½″ long. 56.358

# congo (brazzaville)

Left: *63* Mask. Congo (Brazzaville) or possibly Gabon: Adoumas. Wood, paint, 14⅜″ high. 60.157. Gift of the Matthew T. Mellon Foundation

*66* Funerary figure (Mbulu ngulu). Gabon: Bakota. Wood, copper, brass, 21½″ high. 57.230

# gabon

67  Ghost mask. Gabon, Ogowe River area: Balumbo? Wood, red and white paint, 11⅜″ high. 56.403. Gift of Mr. Eliot Elisofon

68  Mask. Gabon. Wood, white paint, 11¾″ high. 56.343

69 Funerary figure. Gabon: Fang. Wood, 14″ high.
59.104

70 Mask. Congo (Brazzaville): Bakwele. Wood; white, rust and umber paint; 20¾″ high. 56.218

Right: *71* Mask. Congo (Brazzaville): Bakwele. Wood, black, white, and traces of red paint, 30⅛″ high. 56.216

Below: *71a* Mask. Congo (Brazzaville): Bakwele. Wood, black and white paint, 17¼″ high. 57.236

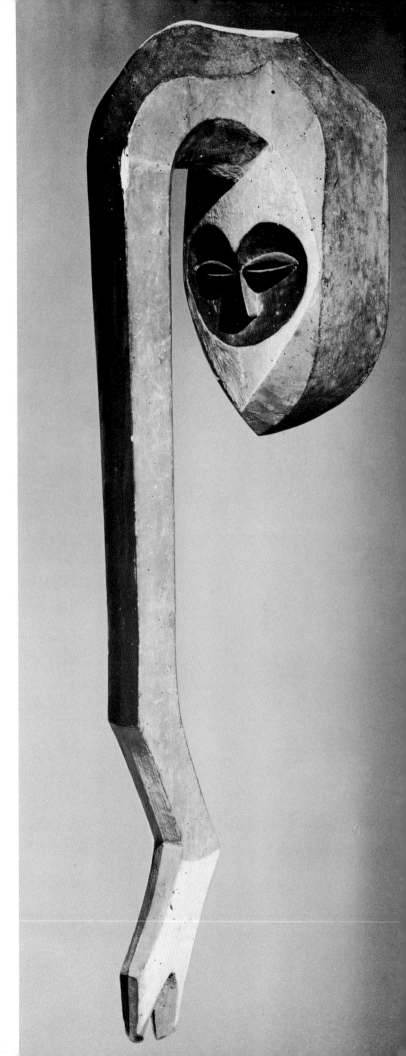

*71b* Mask. Congo (Leopoldville): Baluba. Wood, black and white paint, 14⅝" high. 56.56

# congo
# (leopoldville)

*72* Maternity figure (Ntadi). Congo (Leopoldville): Baboma. Stone, 14¼″ high. 61.47

*73* Stool. Congo (Leopoldville): Baluba. Wood, blue and white beads, 23¼″ high. 58.55

*74* Head. Congo (Leopoldville): Warega. Ivory, cowrie shell, grass, 8½″ high. 57.249

72

73      74

75  Cup. Congo (Leopoldville): Bushongo. Wood, traces of tukula powder, 8¼″ high. 59.7

76  Mask (Kifwebe). Congo (Leopoldville): Basonge. Wood, red and white paint, 17½″ high. 58.171

# central african republic

77  Figure. Central African Republic: Azande. Wood, 7⅞"
high. 61.48